This book belongs to:

_____

Dedicated to my boys,
Drew, Cooper, Wesley and Ford.
To each of you: "I'm so glad you are my son."

GIANT LOVE
Written by Andy Savage and Andrew Chandler
Chief Kid Editor: Drew Savage, Age 7
Illustration by Andrew Chandler
Layout and Project Management by Speak Creative, speakcreative.com

Third Printing

1

I've got a GIANT problem.
I face it every day.
No matter what I do or say,
The GIANTS seem to stay.

These giants each have their own name,
And one by one they come.
Attacking, poking, prodding me,
To do what they have done.

One is named **Dishonesty**,
He really is a pest.
He lies and cheats and steals from you.
At fibbing, he's the best.

The next one is a nuisance.
Disobedience is his name.
He thinks he knows what's best for him,
But never takes the blame.

Defiance is another one
Who won't obey or listen.
He fights and shouts and pouts about.
His thoughts they need adjustin'.

Watch out for this other guy.
He's mighty ugly too.
He's **Disrespectful** all the time
And always mean to you.

4

Separately they're bad enough,
But just you wait and see.
When they're all together,
The **SIN GANG** troubles me.

Their no-good business does me harm.
It knocks me to the ground.
It skins my knees and bumps my head.
It pushes me around.

And when they're done they leave me there,
All broken and alone.
Until another giant comes,
The biggest, baddest one.

This one goes by **Consequence**,
And soon you will see why.
What he does next, I hate to say.
It makes me want to cry.

He wraps me up with ropes and chains,
And ties me to a tree.
But though I strain and struggle hard
I cannot wiggle free.

8

Sin was fun at first, I thought,
But no, not anymore.
I'm in giant trouble now
And feeling scared and sore.

All the good things I have loved
Are kept away from me.
Then I'm sorry that I listened
To those giants, yes-sir-ee.

I hear a noise, a thunderous roar
From far across the way,
Coming down from the mountain,
Someone to save the day?

10

"Of course it's not," growls **Consequence**.
"Pay no attention there.
No one can help to set you free.
Those chains could hold a bear!"

"Besides, your time is almost up.
Your doom is almost here.
You'll pay the price for all your sins.
Your death is very near."

Then I feel him lift me up
And toss me to the wind.
Down into the canyon,
I think my life will end.

13

Just before all was lost
And much to my surprise,
Another giant catches me
I can't believe my eyes!

14

This giant so immense in size,
He holds me in his hand.
I hardly see his top or sides,
He covers all the land.

The chains fall off and I am free,
No more to wind up dead.
He paid the price of consequence
And rescued me instead.

He saved me from the canyon deep
And from that awful tree.
Now I have a giant friend;
He goes everywhere with me.

He fills me with his giant strength
To help me stand my ground.
The **SIN GANG** doesn't stand a chance
When they try to come around.

"Why," I asked my giant friend,
"Did you come down from above?"
He smiled and laughed and said, "Because…
You needed GIANT LOVE."

Understanding GIANT LOVE.
A discussion between a parent and child.

Instructions for Parents: The purpose of the second half of this book is to help your child understand what it means to trust in Jesus as his or her personal Savior and Lord. We encourage you to read the first half of this book several times until you feel your child is ready for this discussion. Read through this part personally before reading it to your child to get a feel for how this discussion may go. When you feel they are ready, take your time and enjoy the discussion. When they are ready to pray the "**GIANT PRAYER**" on page 28 be sure to write it down and use this book as a "scrapbook" for them to remember their decision. We are praying for you as you lead the way for your child to understand God's **GIANT LOVE**.

There is something you need to know. God loves you. In fact, God has **GIANT LOVE** for you. God made you so that He might love you and that you would love Him back.

Can you think of some people who really love you? (Write their names below.)

It may be hard to believe but God loves you even more!
But there is a **GIANT** problem: sin.

Sin is very bad news.

Sin is a little word that means **GIANT** trouble.

You sin when you are **Dishonest**... like when you tell a lie.

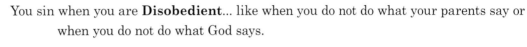

You sin when you are **Disobedient**... like when you do not do what your parents say or when you do not do what God says.

You sin when you are **Defiant**... like when you have bad thoughts or a bad attitude.

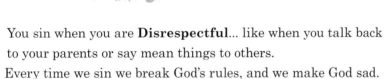

You sin when you are **Disrespectful**... like when you talk back to your parents or say mean things to others.

Every time we sin we break God's rules, and we make God sad.

God is sad because He has **GIANT LOVE** for you, and He knows your sin will hurt you and keep you away from Him.

The Bible says in Romans 3:23, "...all have sinned and fall short of the glory of God." This means no one is perfect, everyone has sinned, everyone is a sinner and everyone does wrong... except God, God is holy and God never sins.

Holy is a Bible word that means "different." God is very different from you, He is perfect, He is not a sinner, He never sins and He is always right.

Disrespect   **Defiance**   **Disobedience**   **Dishonesty**

Do you think you have sinned? Yes or No

Each parent and child: Write down an example of a time when you sinned.

Draw a line from your sin to the member of the **SIN GANG** your sin is most like.

Sin has **GIANT** consequences.

Just like burning your hand is the consequence of touching something hot.
Or getting a bad grade is the consequence of not doing your schoolwork.
Or making people sad is the consequence of being mean.
I'll bet you know how consequences work...

· What is a consequence of not cleaning your room when your parents ask?

· What is a consequence of eating too much candy?

· What is a consequence when you tell a lie?

· What is a consequence of not wearing your seat belt in the car?

A consequence is
something that
happens after we
make a choice.

24

The Bible tells us about two **GIANT** consequences that happen because of our sin...

Consequence #1 – distance

Your sin separates you from God.

It's like there is a **GIANT** canyon separating you and God.

Consequence #2 – death

Your sin deserves to be punished.

The Bible says in Romans 6:23, "The penalty for sin is death..."

That is very scary. It means that you must die to pay for your sins.

You can't pay for your sins by being good or being nice or going to church or reading the Bible or even promising not to sin again. There is nothing you can do to get over to God's side of the canyon.

Isaiah 59:2 "But your iniquities have separated you from your God; your sins have hidden his face from you, so that he will not hear."

This is very bad news.

But, there is **Good News** for this **GIANT** problem...
Do you remember how this story ended?

That's right, **GIANT LOVE!** God loves you and wants to be your friend, but He hates the sin in your life.
God's **GIANT LOVE** is the only thing that can fix the **GIANT** problem of your sin.
God loves you so much, and He showed it in a **GIANT** way.
God sent His only son Jesus into this world.
Jesus was born as a little baby just like you and grew to be a man, but He was different.
He was holy because He was God.

Because Jesus was a man, He could live on our side of the canyon.
Because Jesus was God, He never sinned.
Because He never sinned, He never had to face the consequences of sin.

John 3:16 "For God so loved the world that he gave his one and only Son, that whoever believes in him shall not perish but have eternal life."

Romans 5:8 "But God shows his own love for us in this: While we were still sinners, Christ died for us."

Jesus decided to take your consequences, so you don't have to.
The Bible says Jesus died on the cross to save sinners just like you.
Jesus did what you could not do.
Jesus died in your place. He took your penalty.
His death on the cross was for your sins.

You did the sinning and Jesus took the consequences.

There is more **Good News**!
Jesus died on the cross but God raised Him from the dead.
This is an awesome part of the story.
Jesus' death on the cross means that your sins can be forgiven.
Jesus' resurrection means He is alive today and loves to help people,
like you, become friends with God.
This is what the Bible calls **Salvation**.
Jesus was the **GIANT** that saved us from our
GIANT sin and **GIANT** consequences so we
could be with God, just like God wanted all along.

1 Timothy 1:15	The Bible calls this
"…Christ Jesus came into	resurrection, that's a big
the world to save sinners…"	word that means, he rose
	from the dead.

Becoming A Christian

Do you want to be saved? Here's how you can receive God's **GIANT LOVE**.

1. Tell God you are sorry for your sins.

2. Believe that Jesus died on the cross and rose from the dead to be your Savior.

3. Ask Jesus to forgive you for your sins, to come live in your heart and make you forever friends with God.

4. Thank God for His **GIANT LOVE** and sending Jesus to be your Savior and Lord (boss) of your life.

You might try a **GIANT PRAYER** that goes like this:

Dear God,
I'm sorry for my sins. I believe in my heart that Jesus died
on the cross for me and rose from the dead so I could be forever friends
with You. Please forgive me for my sins. I confess that Jesus is my Lord and
Savior today. Please come into my heart and show me how to live for You.
Thank you for saving me and for your GIANT LOVE for me. In Jesus' name I
pray, AMEN.

After you say this prayer, make sure a grown up knows about your decision.
I prayed the **GIANT PRAYER** on (date) ———————————————.

John 3:16 "...whoever believes in him shall not perish but have eternal life."

Romans 10:13 "Everyone who calls on the name of the Lord will be saved."

Romans 10:9-10 "If you declare with your mouth, "Jesus is Lord," and believe in your heart that God raised him from the dead, you will be saved. For it is with your heart that you believe and are justified, and it is with your mouth that you profess your faith and are saved."

Now That You Are A Christian

All the sins you've ever done or ever will do are forgiven by God, and Jesus is the Lord (boss) of your life.

When you prayed the **GIANT PRAYER**, Jesus gave you a **GIANT** gift. You can't see this gift because it lives in you. This gift is the Holy Spirit. Just like Jesus, the Holy Spirit is different. He is holy, too. He is invisible, but He lives in you so He can remind you of God's **GIANT LOVE** and that Jesus is your boss. So, whenever the **SIN GANG** comes around, you can ask the Holy Spirit to help you remember that you are a Christian and that Jesus is your boss. With the Holy Spirit's help, you can say, "No!" to sin.

Baptism

The next step is for you to be baptized. Don't worry– it's actually pretty easy. Baptism is a very cool way to show your family, friends and church that you believe in Jesus.

How baptism works.

1. Tell your story.
Tell people about the decision you made to believe in Jesus and that Jesus has forgiven you of all your sins and is now the boss of your life. You might want to share some of the things you learned in this book.

2. Go under water.
Going under water for baptism is a great way to show on the outside what Jesus has done on the inside. Getting totally soaked with water in baptism reminds people that you have been totally soaked by God's **GIANT LOVE** and forgiveness.

3. Come out of the water.
This shows everyone that you are going to live for Jesus every day. (Trust me everyone will be super-excited that you made this decision!)

I was baptized on (date) ———————————————.

The Lord's Supper

The Lord's Supper is a very special time when Christians (people who believe Jesus is their Savior) eat a little piece of bread and drink a little sip of grape juice. Jesus told us to do this to remember what He did for us. Now that you are a Christian, you get to eat the bread and drink the juice too.

The bread and the juice remind us of two important things:
1. The bread is a symbol of Jesus' body that was nailed on the cross in your place so you didn't have to die for your sin.
2. The juice is a symbol of Jesus' blood, which is kind of like the soap that washes away our sin and makes us friends with God.

Jesus loved us so much that He gave His own life so that we could be saved. That is **GIANT** news we should never forget. That is why we should always be thankful to Jesus when we take the Lord's Supper.

I took my first Lord's Supper on (date) —————————————————— .

The Lord's Supper is also called Communion or Eucharist (Yu-ka-rist).

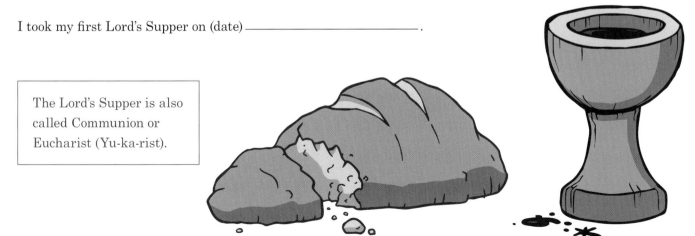

"Parenting is an infinite task with eternal consequences that must be done with finite resources on a limited timeline by imperfect people with virtually no experience who get little thanks, sleep or free time and comes with no second chances."

At Highpoint Church, we believe in helping parents successfully navigate the **7000**Days™ adventure from "crib to college." We call this our **7000**Days™ vision. Through resources, seminars and personal support our prayer is to make your parental journey a little easier. We want you to be equipped and confident for anything and everything from helping your kids take their first steps to understanding their "walk" with God. Please visit us online at **7000**Days.org, highpointmemphis.com and follow us on Twitter @**7000**Days.

If you feel this book was a valuable resource for you, we urge you to consider giving it to a friend or purchasing a copy for someone else on their **7000**Days™ journey. To purchase a copy of *GIANT LOVE*, please visit andysavage.net.

andy savage *making God make sense.*

About the Author
Andy Savage

From teaching to blogging to relationship coaching, Andy strives to live out his life passion of "making God make sense." Andy devotes his time to speaking, writing, coaching parents, and teaching both married couples and single adults the "how-to's" for effective, God-centered relationships.

Andy is the president of Andy Savage Ministries and serves as the teaching pastor at Highpoint Church, a dynamic church in the heart of Memphis, TN, he helped start in 2002. A native Memphian, Andy earned his bachelor's degree in Business Administration from the University of Memphis followed by a Master's degree in Christian Studies from Union University.

Andy is married to his lovely wife Amanda, and they have four children, Drew, Cooper, Wesley and Ford. While Andy spends most of his free time with his family, he is also an avid CrossFitter® and a lover of great coffee.

To learn more about Andy visit: andysavage.net highpointmemphis.com, Twitter: @makesense

About the Illustrator
Andrew Chandler

Andrew seeks to share his gifts with others whenever possible and desires to help people visualize and bring their ideas to reality. Since 2003, Andrew has made Memphis his home and base of operations for his creative endeavors.

Andrew is a graduate of Columbus College of Art and Design. Some of Andrew's clients have included numerous churches and non-profits, Christ Community Health Services, Service Over Self, Memphis Sport Magazine, and Memphis Mayor A.C. Wharton. He has authored and illustrated three children's books and illustrated multiple titles for other authors. He has also logged countless hours as a caricature artist.

He frequently enjoys playing guitar, writing poems, stories, skits and songs, making puppets and costumes, and acting. He loves spending time with his growing family. Andrew is married to his gracious wife Amanda, and has two sons, Noah and Toby, who put up with his ridiculous eccentricities while he merrily freelances from their home.

To learn more about Andrew visit: andrewchandler.net